This book belongs to:

Brooke
Hargrove

DREAM
BELIEVE
ACHIEVE

JoJo Siwa

BuzzPop

An imprint of Little Bee Books
251 Park Avenue South, New York, NY 10010
Copyright © 2017 by Viacom International Inc.
Nickelodeon and all related titles and logos are trademarks
of Viacom International Inc.
JoJo Siwa is a trademark of JoJo Siwa Entertainment, LLC.

BuzzPop and associated colophon
are trademarks of Little Bee Books.
Manufactured in Canada TIG 0819
First Edition

7 9 11 13 15 17 18 16 14 12 10 8
ISBN 978-1-4998-0732-5
buzzpopbooks.com

Contents

There's so much fun inside, including:

BE You

DREAM *Crazy* BIG

7

All About Me

Fill these pages with all the cute, cool, and crazy things about you and your life.

name: ....

nickname: ....

birthday: ....

age: ....

year born: ....

zodiac sign: ....

hometown/city: ....

BFF: ....

pets: ....

SWEET

Most embarrassing moment EVER:

....

....

....

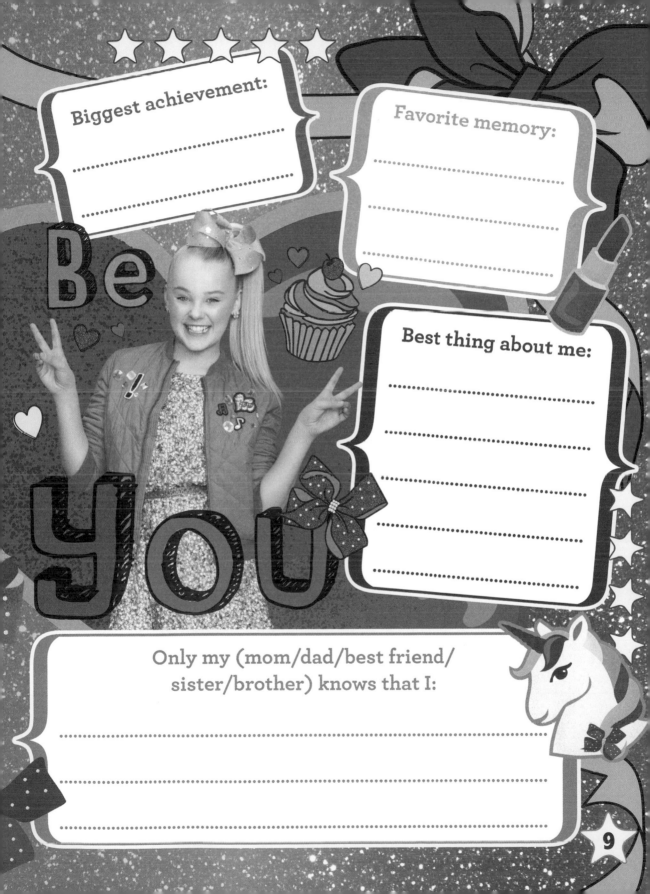

Biggest achievement:

....

....

....

Favorite memory:

....

....

....

....

Best thing about me:

....

....

....

....

....

Only my (mom/dad/best friend/
sister/brother) knows that I:

....

....

....

Fave Things

Fill this page with all your fave things.

friend:...

family member:.....................................

movie:...

TV show:..

vlogger:...

candy bar:..

song: ....

store:..

animal: ....

sport: ....

food:...

drink: ....

time of year:..

day of the week:...................................

The thing I love doing most in the world is:

....

....

....

The first thing I do after I get up is:

....

....

....

....

The best part of the day is when I:

....

....

....

The last thing I do before I go to sleep is:

....

....

....

My Life

★★★★	morning	afternoon	evening
Monday			
Tuesday			
Wednesday			
Thursday			
Friday			
Saturday			
Sunday			

Draw in the clock hands for each time!

Wake up at:

A clock face showing numbers 12, 1, 2, 3, 4, 5, 6, 7, 8, 9, 10, 11

School starts at:

A clock face showing numbers 12, 1, 2, 3, 4, 5, 6, 7, 8, 9, 10, 11

Eat lunch at:

A clock face showing numbers 12, 1, 2, 3, 4, 5, 6, 7, 8, 9, 10, 11

Finish school at:

A clock face showing numbers 12, 1, 2, 3, 4, 5, 6, 7, 8, 9, 10, 11

Eat dinner at:

A clock face showing numbers 12, 1, 2, 3, 4, 5, 6, 7, 8, 9, 10, 11

Go to sleep at:

A clock face showing numbers 12, 1, 2, 3, 4, 5, 6, 7, 8, 9, 10, 11

DID YOU KNOW JOJO'S FAVORITE SUBJECT IS MATH?!

EAT
DANCE
SLEEP

Family Tree

Fill in your family tree with names, pics, or doodles to show who's who in your family.

Who is the cuddliest:
.............JOJO...............

Who is the loudest:
....

Who is the happiest:
....

Who is the messiest:

....

Who is the funniest:

....

Who is the chattiest:

....

Who is the cutest:

....

Who is the smartest:

....

SWEET

BFFs

Which of your pals is your

best friend:

....

kindest friend:

....

funniest friend:

....

oldest friend:

....

Which of your friends is the best dancer:

....

most organized:

....

best shopper:

....

most scatterbrained:

....

WHO IS MOST LIKE JOJO IN YOUR FRIEND GROUP?

BFF Gallery

Fill these pages with pics of you and your BFFs, or doodle your own!

SWEET

SO

I LOVE YOU

JOJO LOVES HER
PET DOG, BOWBOW.
CAN DOGS BE BFFS?
DEFINITELY!

19

Friendship Quiz

Take this quick quiz to find out if you and your friend will be BFFs.

1. How long have you and your pal been friends?

A seems like forever ♡

B a couple of years ♡

C a few months ♡

2. How often do you see your friend?

A every day ♡

B a few times a month ♡

C hardly ever ♡

3. How often do you and your friend have a falling out?

A hardly and just over silly things ♡

B quite often ♡

C we argue most days ♡

4. If your friend had a bad hair day, what would you do?

A help her restyle it ♡

B lend her a hat to cover it up ♡

C refuse to be seen with her ♡

5.

Have you ever forgotten your friend's birthday?

A   never, it's written in my planner ♡

B   sometimes, but I always
make it up to them ♡

C   I forget every year ♡

6.

Do you keep your friend's secrets?

A   always ♡

B   usually, unless I forget and tell
someone by mistake ♡

C   sometimes, but I often end up
telling other friends too ♡

7.

If your friend copies you, what do you do?

A   laugh, but like that we're
the same ♡

B   feel embarrassed, but try to
ignore it ♡

C   get really mad and tell her to stop ♡

DISCOVER YOUR
RATING ON THE
NEXT PAGE!

Friendship *Quiz*

How did you do?

Mostly As

You and your friend are two of a kind and will be best friends forever!

Mostly Bs

You're great pals, but you like to hang out with other friends too.

Mostly Cs

Hmmm, sounds like you're good friends, but not best friends.

JOJO LOVES HAVING HER FRIENDS JOIN HER ON HER YOUTUBE CHANNEL.

Odd Cupcake Out

Which one of these cupcakes isn't like the rest?
Can you spot the odd one out?

See answer on page 84

Word Power

Which of these JoJo-inspired words describe you?
Check off as many as you want!

Sweet

Confident

Positive

Awesome

Crazy

Happy

Dreamer

Loyal

Funny

Super

Hopeful

Chill

Energetic

Achiever

DREAM CRAZY BIG

Bow Crazy

Count all the bows on these pages.
How many can you count of each design?

See answers on page 84 27

Seek and Find

Can you spot all the cute words
below in the puzzle?

SWEET

PUFF

GIGGLE

TWINKLE

WARM

CUDDLE

SPARKLE

CUTE

FLUFFY

BOWBOW

W	B	C	U	D	D	L	E	K	M	P	V
X	B	R	H	G	L	A	Y	R	Q	O	F
T	A	O	F	M	U	N	A	X	W	D	B
W	Z	E	W	I	T	W	D	L	S	K	S
I	F	K	C	B	M	E	Z	R	C	U	P
N	L	D	W	Q	O	T	D	B	U	S	A
K	P	X	N	U	S	W	E	E	T	G	R
L	W	T	R	Y	I	A	X	J	E	M	K
E	N	G	J	P	O	C	T	Y	L	E	L
J	T	W	A	U	E	G	I	G	G	L	E
F	L	U	F	F	Y	I	P	Z	H	J	P
D	F	I	S	F	Z	G	J	E	P	W	I

SUPER CUTE

See answers on page 84

Animal Cuties

JoJo loves her cute dog, BowBow! Number the animals on these pages from 1 to 20, with 1 for the cutest and 20 for the least cute.

Panda

Elephant

Piglet

Duckling

Kitten

Puppy

Mouse

Owl

Squirrel

Chick

Whale

Shark

Ladybug

Bumblebee

Monkey

Worm

Seal

Hedgehog

Goldfish

Parrot

31

JoJo Spotting

These small pictures of JoJo may look the same as the big picture, but something is different in each one. Can you spot the differences? Circle each one.

a.

b.

c.

d.

Cutie Cut-outs

Cut out all the cute pics on the following pages and use them to decorate your notebook, diary, bedroom, or school locker.

BOWS MAKE EVERYTHING BETTER

DREAM **Crazy** BIG

CUTE & CONFIDENT

Super Cute

This book belongs to:

This book belongs to:

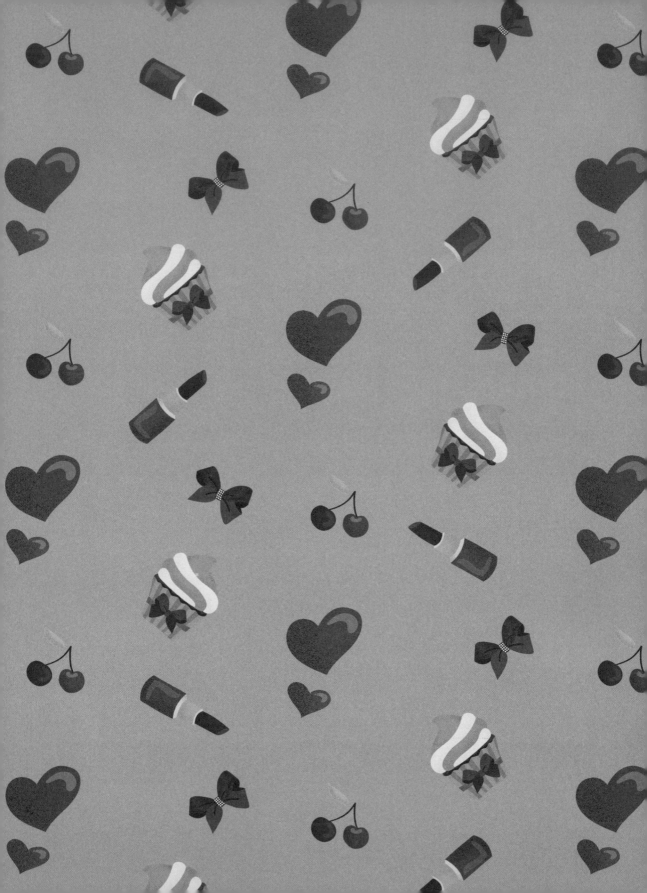

TOP SECRET!

TOP SECRET!

TOP SECRET!

I ♥ my BFF

I ♥ my BFF

I ♥ my BFF

DO NOT DISTURB

DO NOT DISTURB

DO NOT DISTURB

Chill Out!

Chill Out!

Chill Out!

BE You

BE You

BE You

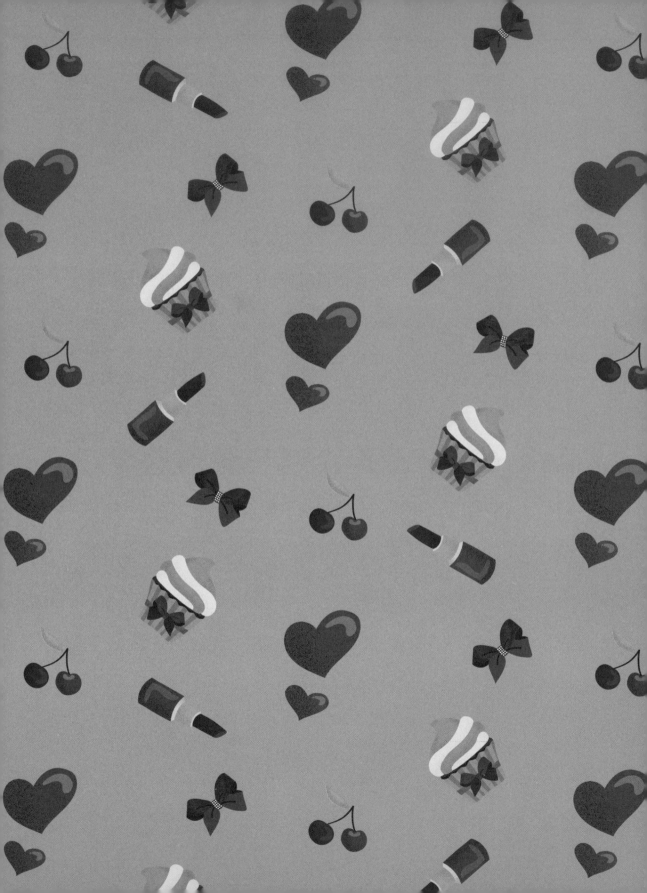

Sweet Tweets!

Check out these JoJo-inspired hashtags, then write your own below.

#BestiesNotBullies
#PeaceOutHaterz
#JoJosJuice

ASK A PARENT OR GUARDIAN'S PERMISSION BEFORE POSTING ONLINE.

\# ....

\# ....

\# ....

\# ....

\# ....

\# ....

\# ....

\# ....

\# ....

\# ....

JoJo's Juice

Vlog It?

If you could have your own YouTube channel just like JoJo, what would you vlog about? Come up with some super-awesome ideas that are important to you.

1.

Vlog idea:..

Main points to talk about:....................................

....

Props needed:..

2.

Vlog idea:..

Main points to talk about:....................................

....

Props needed:..

3.

Vlog idea:..

Main points to talk about:....................................

....

Props needed:..

ASK A PARENT OR GUARDIAN'S PERMISSION BEFORE POSTING ONLINE.

4.

Vlog idea:..

Main points to talk about:...

....

Props needed:..

5.

Vlog idea:..

Main points to talk about:...

....

Props needed:..

DID YOU KNOW THAT JOJO ENDS EVERY VLOG BY POURING JUICE OVER HER HEAD? THAT'S WHY HER CHANNEL IS CALLED JOJO'S JUICE.

JOJO'S JUICE

41

House Tour!

JoJo loves telling her fans all about her life!

Draw your home in this frame and label your favorite parts.

Write down five awesome facts about your home:

1. ....

2. ....

3. ....

4. ....

5. ....

Closet Cool

What does your dream closet look like? Draw it below and organize your clothes and accessories!

DID YOU SEE JOJO'S CLOSET TOUR VLOG?

Will you organize by color or type?

Fave Foods!

List all your favorite foods on this page! Who would you invite to your dream dinner party? (JoJo, of course!)

Favorite fruits:..

....

Favorite vegetables:...

....

Lunch box essentials: ....

....

Favorite snacks: ....

....

Favorite international foods: ....

....

Foods I want to try:...

Favorite foods to share: ....

 46

DREAM Crazy BIG

JoJo has always tried to follow her dreams and achieve her goals! She tells everyone to dream crazy big! In this section write down your hopes and dreams for the future.

_____

_____

_____

_____

_____

_____

_____

WHY NOT TAPE THIS SECTION TOGETHER, THEN OPEN IT UP AGAIN IN THE FUTURE AND SEE IF YOUR DREAMS CAME TRUE?

47

Daydreamer

school

clothes

friends

vacations

celebs

food

ghosts

TV shows

movies

dancing

family

pets

48

Dream Home

My dream home would be a/an:

mansion ♡

castle ♡

apartment ♡

ranch ♡

farm ♡

yacht ♡

mobile home ♡

beach house ♡

My dream home would be:

next door to my BFF ♡

around the corner from where I live now ♡

up on a mountain ♡

on a beach ♡

on a lake ♡

next to a river ♡

in a forest ♡

in the countryside ♡

Doodle your fave daydream in this bubble.

My dream home would be in:

Europe ♡

Asia ♡

Australia ♡

North America ♡

South America ♡

Africa ♡

Antarctica ♡

The Arctic ♡

Dream Vacation

What would your dream vacation be like?

My dream vacation would be in:

Europe ♡
Asia ♡
Australia ♡
North America ♡
South America ♡
Africa ♡
Antarctica ♡
The Arctic ♡

I would travel by:

bike ♡
boat ♡
plane ♡
helicopter ♡
car ♡
submarine ♡

I would stay in a/an:

hotel ♡
RV ♡
apartment ♡
castle ♡

I would eat:

fruit ♡
pizza ♡
ice cream ♡
sweets ♡

Dream Job

What would your dream job be?

I would love to work with:

animals ♡

children ♡

only my friends ♡

on my own ♡

I would love to work:

in an office ♡

in a dance studio ♡

on the beach ♡

in a garden ♡

in a shop ♡

in a vehicle ♡

in a foreign country ♡

in outer space ♡

in the jungle ♡

Number these jobs from 1 to 12, with 1 being the one you'd most like to do, and 12 the least.

vet

teacher

doctor

astronaut

news anchor

vlogger

dancer

actor

engineer

marine biologist

firefighter

pilot

Decode Your Dreams!

Ever wondered what your dreams mean? Write about the last dream you remember below. Was it weird, crazy, scary, exciting, or fun?

....

....

....

....

....

....

....

....

....

....

....

....

If you dream you are FALLING from the sky, down a hole, or off a cliff, it can mean you feel out of control. Try to work out what area of your life you need to take control of, and what you can do about it.

If you dream you are FLYING, it means you feel confident, secure about your life, and in control. If you dream you are flying too high, it can mean you are concerned how your success might change your life.

If you dream you are BEING CHASED, it means you have a problem in your life that you need to face up to and deal with.

WHATEVER YOUR DREAMS MIGHT MEAN, REMEMBER TO DREAM BIG, JUST LIKE JOJO!

Your Dream Year

What do you want to achieve in the next year? Write down your goals and dreams for the future.

January

....

....

....

February

....

....

....

March

....

....

....

April

....

....

....

May

....

....

....

June

....

....

....

July

....

....

....

August

....

....

....

September

....

....

....

October

....

....

....

November

....

....

....

December

....

....

....

My Future

In 1 year, I hope: ....

....

....

....

....

....

In 3 years, I hope: ....

....

....

....

....

In 5 years, I hope:...
....
....
....
....
....

In 10 years, I hope:...
....
....
....
....
....

NOW SEAL THIS SECTION WITH TAPE AND
OPEN IT AGAIN IN THE FUTURE!

Copy Draw

Draw the picture on the left in the grid on the right.

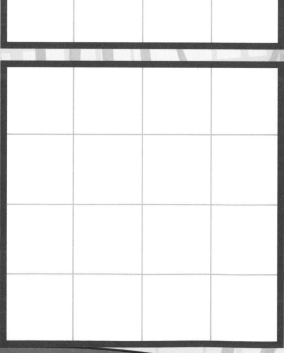

Rule the School!

Fill this page with all your fave things about your school!

name of your school:

....

fave subject:..

fave teacher: ....

most amazing thing you've

learned this year: ....

....

....

....

Number these subjects from 1 to 10, with 1 being your most fave subject and 10 your least.

English

Science

Drama

Math

Geography

Gym

History

Music

Art

Foreign Language

Use the space above to design a super-cute school uniform.

DON'T FORGET YOUR SCHOOL BAG!

Jumbled Lines

Hurry, JoJo needs juice for her latest vlog! Which line leads her to the juice?

a.

b.

c.

SWEET

JoJo's Juice

JoJo's JUICE

Happy Holidays

Check off which type of vacation you've been on and circle the ones you'd love to try!

camping

beach

sightseeing

safari

adventure

diving

skiing

cooking

horseback riding

Other:

....

....

cruise

....

....

cycling

....

Best vacation memory ever:

....

....

If you could go on vacation with anyone, you would go with:

....

....

Worst vacation memory ever:

....

....

Name three places you have been to on vacation:

....

....

....

Name three places you would love to go on vacation:

....

....

....

Get ready for your next vacation with your top 5 items to pack:

....

....

....

....

....

Design your own cute suitcase to take on your next vacation.

Create Your Own Blog

Use the spaces on these pages to plan your own blog or website, just like JoJo's.

Step 1 — Think of a name or handle for your site:

www...

@ ....

Step 2 — Design a logo and your masthead (the picture at the top of your site):

Step 3 What kind of things would you blog about?

fashion

books

politics

art

friends

animals

news

movies

music

travel

other:
....

TV shows

Step 4

How often will you post?

every day

once a week

once a month

DON'T FORGET
TO ALWAYS ASK A
GROWN-UP BEFORE
YOU GO ONLINE!

Step 5

Make sure you include popular hashtags to help share your content:

#...

#...

#...

Step 6

Decide who you will share your blog with and ask them to rate it from 1 to 10.

family

friends

teachers

Fashion Update

Which of the items below do you want to add to your wardrobe?

If you did a JoJo-inspired fashion update, which clothes would be on your fashion hit list? Create your dream haul on these pages.

jeans ✓

shorts ✓

sweatpants ✓

dress ✓

sweater ✓

miniskirt ✓

corduroys ✓

maxi skirt ✓

jacket ✓

skirt ✓

leggings ✓

pants ✓

blazer ✓

T-shirt ✓

hat ✓

Check off all the colors you love to wear:

Where do you like to shop for...?

something fancy:

....

chill-out clothes:

....

sportswear:

....

accessories:

....

something different:

....

DID YOU KNOW JOJO'S FAVORITE COLOR IS PINK SPARKLE?

Design your dream outfit in this box:

JOJO HAS HER OWN UNIQUE SENSE OF STYLE! HOW WOULD YOU DESCRIBE YOURS?

My Routine

Fill out the chart to discover more about your routine. How often do you do the following?

	twice a day	every day	twice a week	once a week	once a month	never
wash your hair						
brush your hair						
brush your teeth						
get a haircut						
paint your nails						
take a selfie						
hang with your BFF						
watch TV						
play a video game						
go for a walk						
exercise						
learn a new fact						
dream about the future						

What are your good habits?

....

....

....

....

....

JOJO PRACTICES DANCE ROUTINES MOST DAYS A WEEK!

EAT DANCE SLEEP

Do you have any bad habits?

....

....

....

....

....

Perfect Pairs!

Can you draw lines between all the pairs that match?

See answers on page 85

Happy Birthday!

Never forget a friend's birthday again. Write down the birthdays of your loved ones on these pages.

name:...

birthday:...

age:..

zodiac sign:...

perfect present:

....

....

perfect present:

....

....

name:...

birthday:...

age:..

zodiac sign:...

name:...

birthday:...

age:..

zodiac sign:...

perfect present:

....

....

perfect present:
....
....

name:...
birthday:..
age: ....
zodiac sign:..

name:...
birthday:..
age:...
zodiac sign:..

perfect present:
....
....

perfect present:
....
....

name:...
birthday:..
age:...
zodiac sign:..

name:...
birthday:..
age:...
zodiac sign:..

perfect present:
....
....

perfect present:
....
....

name:............................
birthday:............................
age:............................
zodiac sign:............................

name:............................
birthday:............................
age:............................
zodiac sign:............................

perfect present:
....
....

perfect present:
....
....

name:............................
birthday:............................
age:............................
zodiac sign:............................

name:............................
birthday:............................
age:............................
zodiac sign:............................

perfect present:
....
....

perfect present:

....

....

name: ....

birthday: ....

age: ....

zodiac sign: ....

name: ....

birthday: ....

age: ....

zodiac sign: ....

perfect present:

....

....

perfect present:

....

....

name: ....

birthday: ....

age: ....

zodiac sign: ....

DON'T FORGET JOJO'S BIRTHDAY!

name: JOJO SIWA

birthday: MAY 19, 2003

age: ....

zodiac sign: TAURUS

perfect present: BOWS, OBVIOUSLY!

Coloring Competition

Color all the cute stuff on these pages. Ask each of your friends to color in something, then pick your favorite!

From My Heart To Yours

SUPER CUTE

BE YOUR OWN Star

79

Bow Designer

JoJo has so many bows because

BOWS ARE EVERYTHING!

Design JoJo a new bow on the template below, then design one for yourself on the opposite page.

BOWS ARE MY SUPER POWER

DID YOU KNOW JOJO HAS NEARLY 1,000 BOWS?! WHOA!

Fan Mail

JoJo loves getting fan mail! Write a letter to her on this page. Ask a parent or guardian to share your letter on social media @itsjojosiwa.

Dear JoJo,

Answers

Page 23

a.

b.

c.

d.

e.

f.

Pages 26–27

 2

 4

 3

 6

 3

 5

Pages 28–29

W	B	C	U	D	D	L	E	K	M	P	V
X	B	R	H	G	L	A	Y	R	Q	O	F
T	A	O	F	M	U	N	A	X	W	D	B
W	Z	E	W	I	T	W	D	L	S	K	S
I	F	K	C	B	M	E	Z	R	C	U	P
N	L	D	W	Q	O	T	D	B	U	S	A
K	P	X	N	U	S	W	E	E	T	G	R
L	W	T	R	Y	I	A	X	J	E	M	K
E	N	G	J	P	O	C	T	Y	L	E	L
J	T	W	A	U	E	G	I	G	G	L	E
F	L	U	F	F	Y	I	P	Z	H	J	P
D	F	I	S	F	Z	G	J	E	P	W	I

Pages 32–33

a.

b.

c.

d.

Pages 62–63

a.
b.
c.

Pages 72–73